P9-CNE-344

HARRISBURG
Renaissance of a Capital City

HANOVER
PUBLIC
LIBRARY

PERPETUAL MEMORIAL

WITHDRAWN

By Guthrie Memorial Library
Hanover's Public Library

In Memory of

HIS GRANDMOTHER

E. M. GITT

FRONT COVER: *Harrisburg's Market Square and Market Street boosts six major recent construction projects including the Whitaker Center for Science and the Arts, the Hilton Harrisburg Towers, and the Penn National Insurance building.* THIS PAGE: *The lighted fountain of the East Capitol plaza glows at dusk.*

HARRISBURG
Renaissance of a Capital City

Photography ©1999 by Blair Seitz
Photography, pages 10 and 11 © The Patriot-News Co.
Text ©1999 by Stephen R. Reed, Janice R. Black, Nathaniel Gadsden, David J. Morrison,
Tina Manoogian-King, Norman Lacasse, Carrie Wissler-Thomas, David Schwartz,
John G. Hope and Ruth Hoover Seitz

ISBN 1-879441-99-3

Library of Congress Catalog Card Number 99-075880

All rights reserved. No part of this book may be reproduced or transmitted in any form or by any
means, electronic or mechanical, including photocopying, recording or by an information storage or
retrieval system without written permission from the authors, photographers and publisher except
for inclusion of brief quotations in a review.

Published by

RB BOOKS ™

"...richly beautiful"

and Seitz, Inc.
6 N. Second St.
burg, Pa 17102-3121
717-232-7944

www.celebratePA.com

Design and prepress by Jednota Commercial Printers, Middletown, Pa 17057
Printed in Hong Kong by Regent Publishing Services, Ltd., St. Louis, Mo 63123.

PHOTO: The Central Pennsylvania Youth Ballet performs at the Rose Lehrman
Performing Arts Center, Harrisburg Area Community College.

HARRISBURG
Renaissance of a Capital City

RB

BOOKS

"...richly beautiful"

Photography by Blair Seitz
Introduction by Janice R. Black
Foreword by Stephen R. Reed

A project of Historic Harrisburg Association

917.48

FOREWORD

by Stephen R. Reed, Mayor, City of Harrisburg

With the dawning of the 21st century, the City of Harrisburg commemorates not only the arrival of a new millennium, but also the arrival of the next stage of its historic renaissance.

Harrisburg is a study in American social history and dynamics. Its progress in the current era chronicles the ardor and effort that answer the question of whether America's cities will have a vibrant place in the nation's future. What has been happening in Pennsylvania's Capital City gives vision and inspiration to not only its own citizens and succeeding generations, but to other urban communities as well.

Because of a listing as the second most distressed city in the United States at the start of the 1980s, conventional wisdom of that time had written-off the city, a self-fulfilling prophecy and a prescription for the worst in economic and social decline. The city was on the verge of bankruptcy. Vast areas were desolate and abandoned. More than half of the downtown was vacant. Harrisburg was dying under the crush of skyrocketing unemployment, crime, collapsing property values, and a failure to sustain even the most basic aspects of community livability.

That was then. This is now. Amidst an initial chorus of skepticism and cynicism, major initiatives launched in the first half of the 1980s were based on three priorities that remain the city's focus: economic development, creation of non-tax revenue sources, and engaging in a constant effort to refine and improve how the government functions.

Nearly 30 years of serious decline could not be reversed by any one project or policy, nor by any quick, overnight solution. Others had tried that and failed. Instead, a long-term strategy was set in place that has produced highly visible results. Theories and concepts about producing urban renewal abound. But few of them relate to the practical realities of replacing blight with restorative investment.

In an age when suburban sprawl creates new construction in former farmlands, forests, and open space, the perception was that older buildings are a city's bane. Harrisburg made them a strength. Seven National Historic Districts have been named. Next to Philadelphia, Harrisburg has the second highest volume of certified historic rehabilitation of any Pennsylvania community. The city's architectural heritage is now commemorated for its richness.

Harrisburg once was an embarrassment for the region, and tourism a dismissable prospect for the city. Today, Harrisburg has regained its role as the regional hub for commerce, finance, history, recreation, sports, and the arts. Tourism is now a very measurable part of its economy.

Statistics cannot tell a total story, but they do give an economic and social measure of the past and present.

Since 1982, more than $2.25 billion in new investment has taken place. More than 23,000 building permits have been issued for projects great and small. In the second half of the 1990s, new records for the number of permits issued annually repeatedly have been set one year and broken the next. Most of this investment has occurred outside of the downtown, while

ABOVE: *The Penn National Insurance building on Market Square rises above the James McCormick Mansion and the Georgian-revival Dauphin County Library (right) at North Front and Walnut Sts.*
RIGHT: *Named for the late US Rep. John Crain Kunkel and Katherine Smoot Kunkel, the Kunkel Memorial Plaza at North Front and State Sts. is site of the sculpture "Waiting" by J. Seward Johnson, Jr.*

the downtown itself clearly has taken on a major new life and a new skyline.

The number of businesses on the city's tax rolls in 1981 was 1,908. Today, it is more than 5,900. The tax base, assessed at $212 million in 1982, today is listed at more than $920 million.

The crime rate has dropped by more than 50%, and the fire rate is down by more than 70% to the lowest level since records have been kept.

Twenty percent more city residents are employed full-time. The unemployment rate, once in double digits, is at its lowest level in 30 years.

The number of vacant structures has declined by 85%. City programs have directly seen to the restoration or new construction of more than 4,500 residential units, while the investment of private developers and home buyers account for many more. The back-to-the-city movement of young professionals, primarily 23 to 40 years old, is adding considerably to the new life in many neighborhoods.

Harrisburg today has the largest municipal parks system of any community in central Pennsylvania, and is host to the region every day. City Island, one of the 27 parks and playgrounds city-wide, attracts more than 1.6 million visitors annually.

The city's special events program, initiated in 1984, now entices more than 2 million visitors yearly, with activities ranging from the American MusicFest during the Independence Day weekend and the Kipona Festival over the Labor Day weekend to neighborhood celebrations and concerts in Italian Lake and Reservoir Parks.

With an emphasis on arts, culture, and history, Harrisburg and its partners have seen to creation of the Whitaker Center for Science and the Arts, the National Civil War Museum, the Greater Harrisburg Fire Museum, arts facilities at Reservoir Park and grand plazas, foun-

tains, and gardens, accented with public art, at multiple sites.

The fervor of sports has returned, with the AA minor league professional baseball franchise, the Harrisburg Senators, home-based at RiverSide Stadium on City Island, a facility first built in 1987 and expanded three times since. The Harrisburg Heat of the National Professional Soccer League hold court at the Farm Show Arena, while the minor league football national champion Central Pennsylvania Piranha can be seen at City Island's Skyline Sports Complex.

Less seen but nevertheless critical to the city's future has been major new investment in the water, sewer, stormwater, bridge, and highway systems, making Harrisburg capable of fully serving present residents and businesses and future growth.

This progress occurred as the city quietly developed entrepreneurial projects to generate non-tax revenues involving trash collection and disposal, steam generation, and electrical co-generation, among others. As a result, today less than 20% of the entire city budget comes from taxes. And since 1987 there have been no city tax increases.

In the post-1982 era, Harrisburg twice has been named an All-America City. It achieved national police accreditation, the highest recognition in the nation for law enforcement operations and a rating that fewer than 500 of the nation's 21,000 police agencies have achieved. Annually, for more than a decade, the city has consistently received the top national awards for budgeting, accounting, and financial reporting. The city's flood preparedness efforts garnered three upgraded ratings from the federal government, a ranking held by only three other communities nationwide, that reduced flood insurance premiums for city property owners. Harrisburg has been separately honored with top awards from the U.S. Environmental Protection Agency, the Arbor Day Foundation, the state Chamber of Business and Industry, and many others. This recognition is an independent assessment of what has evolved in this once colonial crossroads.

The Harrisburg of today is a city of history and heritage, of art and culture, with a modern spirit that embraces the future with vision and confidence. It is a community of contrasts and diversity, like America itself, that has undergone a resurgence in spirit, pride, and amenity.

Poised to build on the progress achieved in the current era, Harrisburg has much to celebrate...and to offer. *H*

ACKNOWLEDGEMENTS

The inspiration for this book came from my friend, George Beyer, an historian at the PA Historical and Museum Commission. George is fond of the early 1900's City Beautiful Movement and urged doing a book on the city's parks and gardens. Since then, in the three years that the book has taken shape, it has become a cooperative effort of the City, the arts community, the neighborhood centers, the supporters of historic preservation and RB Books. With this support RB Books became committed to publishing a book as our contribution to ENVISION Capital Region.

David J. Morrison, Executive Director of Historic Harrisburg when I first discussed the project with him, became an enthusiastic supporter and advisor. Carrie Wissler-Thomas, President of the Art Association of Harrisburg joined David to advise me and make many invaluable suggestions and help with arrangements for the arts' photography. I am deeply indebted to Carrie and David for their generous assistance and support.

The project received a huge boost with Mayor Reed's endorsement, and offering of the support of the City of Harrisburg. I am grateful for assistance given to the project by the City's Parks and Recreation and its Director, Tina Manoogian-King.

The editor for the essays in the book is John J. Hope. Thanks, John, for working the editing into your busy schedule.

Without the calm under pressure exhibited by Jednota Press staff, the book could not have been produced in the two months required. I especially thank Tammy Miller, Betsy Snyder and Eric Baum for their fine work and many hours of overtime.

I photographed over 25 arts groups supported by Allied Arts Fund and The Greater Harrisburg Foundation for the book. I received enthusiastic accommodation by each of the groups for which I am grateful. Both Allied Arts and MetroArts were very helpful in arranging for the photographs. The Whitaker Center was in the last days of preparation for their grand opening when I photographed it. I thank Cynthia A. Sudor, Director of Marketing, and Susan L. Stuart, Director of Development at the Center, for assistance with this project in the midst of a flurry of activities.

I am grateful for the interest and assistance of Ted Martin, Executive Director, Historic Harrisburg Association. The Harrisburg Renaissance Fund established by the Greater Harrisburg Foundation will award benefits from the net proceeds from the sale of the book to the Art Association of Harrisburg, Historic Harrisburg Association and the Wednesday Club.

–Blair Seitz, Photographer/publisher

TABLE OF CONTENTS

LEFT: *Fishing is a favorite Harrisburg leisure activity in Riverfront Park along the Susquehanna River.* RIGHT: *The Kwanzan cherry tree blossoms at the State Museum and State Archives on North 3rd Street are part of Harrisburg springtime beauty.*

by Janice R. Black, President/CEO, The Greater Harrisburg Foundation

Once only a crossroads by the Susquehanna, Harrisburg has evolved into a thriving, cosmopolitan city that still manages to retain a small town friendliness and strong sense of community. We are blessed to live, work, and play in such a magnificent area with recreation and entertainment of all descriptions readily available. Our city is diverse, not only demographically, but also in terms of cultural opportunities. How many other cities have achieved the advantages of a well-developed, first class performing and visual arts community; home for several major corporations; and dedication to urban renewal and historical preservation efforts, and maintain a community spirit that is generally associated with small towns?

Harrisburg today is a tribute to many years of philanthropic giving, volunteer work, and community cooperation. The city's residents and surrounding neighbors exemplify a strong sense of caring, each of us finding ways to contribute to our community–not only with our financial resources, but also our talents and time. As President/CEO of the community foundation for the region, I can give personal witness to the generous commitment of our businesses and individuals in their support of all things Harrisburg: the arts,

historical preservation, and neighborhood development. Although there are groups and individuals who stand out over the years as leaders in this effort, it is wonderfully satisfying to note the influx of new contributors to the health and well-being of Harrisburg. Mayor Reed's vision and encouragement to others to form viable organizations working toward the mutual goal of growing the city is planting seeds today for future harvest. Collectively, we are making Harrisburg a better place.

Harrisburg: Renaissance of a Capital City is a prime example of the group effort required to catapult our city into the next era. The collaborative effort of so many organizations and individuals to celebrate the successes that we enjoy today is astonishing. Greatly enhanced by the breadth of experience and support contributed to the whole, the book is a fitting portfolio of where we are now and serves as inspiration as we go forward. H

Our Beloved Community
by Nathaniel J. Gadsden
Poet Laureate for the City of Harrisburg

*Presented January 5, 1998, on the occasion of the inauguration of the
    Honorable Stephen R. Reed, Mayor of the City of Harrisburg*

Harrisburg, the sun shines bright here when it wants to.
The moon makes shadows upon the Susquehanna
        and the stars give guidance for all that can read them.
The wind is gentle and welcoming at times—and harsh too often.
The waters rise and fall and tell tales old folks remember and talk
        about all the time.
The people move to a beat that's a little off key—sort of country and
        urban funk and jazz.
A select few mark time to a classical meter, while some mark time with
        the blues.
This place is little America—The Burg—Harrisburg, Pennsylvania.

This place is home for many and a way station to some.

This place is not different or strange.

Nature plays no favorites here. The elements are worldly/universal/prescribed.

The ingredients are God's recipe for humanity.

Like a good meal, the ingredients are different but delightful when served together.

This is the Beloved Community.

Together all things work for good. This is a universal story line—a mystery.

Together we solve puzzles that are so large no one person can count all the pieces.

Together we create windows so clear that looking out and looking in is easy
    and pleasant.

Together we build stair steps and pathways large enough for everyone to
    move forward and step up.

Together we lift up candles that illuminate and give vision to all roads and
    bridges that might separate us.

This is Harrisburg, Pennsylvania.

The children make us smile here—and yes
    there are times we cry deep melodies.

Our children hold watch.

They join together with the youthful spirit that we once all knew—looking at
    us—looking at them. They laugh at us and they make us laugh. We love
    to hear our children laughing.

Maybe we are strange but we are not different.

Our elders take us to family reunions on a daily basis.

They use words and faded photos to unite us—the whole of us to home.

They laugh at us and they make us laugh. We see God's handy work
    when the elders laugh.

This is America, the place we keep hearing about.

This is it. Whatever it is supposed to be. Whatever you make it. Whatever
    you call it.

This is the Burg, Harrisburg, the City, the Capital.

Not that big, but not too small.

It's all right here. The sounds, the taste, and the feelings. Every thought
    and every political opinion is here. The religions are here.

Harrisburg, Pennsylvania.

Home to the children of many nations.

The universal home.

Home.

America's home.

Home to all that come.

Together we can do anything.

Harrisburg/together/we can do anything.

Oh yes, We- Yes, We- Yes Yes- We can do anything together,
    Harrisburg.

Especially when we sing love songs that allow everyone to take part and
    causes even God to smile. *H*

Opportunities abound in Harrisburg
for learning and training in the visual
and performing arts.

HARRISBURG VIEWS *Photo Essay by Gary Dwight Miller*

Gary Dwight Miller is a senior staff photographer at the Patriot-News Co. photos © by the Patriot-News. Co.

TOP LEFT: *Rev. Hal Fox, a Shipoke resident braves the snow with Smutty.* TOP RIGHT: *Pastor Harold Lefever conducts summer Bible School at Herr St. Mennonite Church.* FAR LEFT TOP: *"Candles on the Water" night commemorates Hiroshima and Nagasaki.* FAR LEFT BOTTOM: *A kiss is offered by Chanaya Bridges as her friend Torrance Owens pulls back at the Pride of the Neighborhood Academies, Inc. special kindergarten "prom."* LEFT: *At Hamilton Elementary School, cub scouts pledge the flag.*

FAR LEFT: *Franklin Co. 4-H members socialize at the PA Farm Show.* **LEFT:** *The Reservoir Park Sculpture,* Park Mother, *by Deborah Masters has a youthful admirer.* **BELOW LEFT:** *The closing hurrah is given at the square dance at the PA State Farm Show.* **BELOW:** *Kirk Smallwood, head coach of the championship Harrisburg High School basketball team watches a Junior Varsity game with his players.*

Chapter 1

The City I Love
by Nathaniel Gadsden

Nathaniel Gadsden is founder and director of Nathaniel Gadsden's Writer's Wordshop

Born and raised in Harrisburg, I have always loved this city—its simplicity flavored and scented with the potpourri of multiculturalism, a city boasting an unruffled, laid-back nature. Juxtaposed with its casual atmosphere is its nimble pace. As the seat of state government, there is constant brisk activity, always some issue — typically several — under discussion and debate.

Those who know Harrisburg recognize it is easy to love for its festive and fun characteristics and easy to appreciate for its vast arts availability, a place that expediently befits the pursuit of business opportunities and academia. Behold our Susquehanna. The river can be interestingly tricky, at once a source of

beauty and comfort leveled at times to accommodate those who sail, yet never forgotten as the mighty force that has raged and flooded in past years.

To me the Susquehanna is a source of beauty, but also a great divide, a separation between the races, with the urban and inner city of Harrisburg on the river's east shore peppered by various shades of brown, while its west shore is occupied predominantly with hues of white. Even so, the sum of what makes the Susquehanna beautiful attracts us all, so that we join together often at the river to celebrate

ABOVE: *Clowns from Tall Cedars, engage children in games at an Uptown Reel Street block party organized as part of an open house for four renovated homes.* **RIGHT:** *On a City Island baseball diamond close to the AA professional Harrisburg Senators field, a young, aspiring player receives batting tips.*

the city and all it yields. To witness the aesthetics of the Susquehanna is to acquiesce and acknowledge that God is still in charge.

Having grown up in Harrisburg and lived here all my life, I cannot help but recognize the changes and progressions in the city, in myself, and in others. When I was a child being raised on public assistance, there was little money and little else. Yet there always has been an endless list of people and agencies there for me and those like me who needed an extra and very firm push. I am thankful for having been graduated from college and become a productive contributor to the community, aided by affirmative action, positive exchanges, and opportunities designed to empower those who needed it most, and supported by the city's business and religious communities.

Among the greatest joys of my life in Harrisburg has been creation of Nathaniel Gadsden's Writer's Wordshop. Over the past 22 years since its inception, those who have participated have been both renowned word-artists who shared with us and novice writers searching for a platform so their works might be heard and even published. I continue to enjoy each of the individuals who arrive at Wordshop sessions.

I directly attribute my success to my loving wife and partner, Patricia, who is my foundation and the light of my life, and our six children, each of them unique. Pat also loves Harrisburg and established her own business here, Life Esteem. For our wonderful friends and associates, we count ourselves fortunate and well-blessed. *H*

FAR RIGHT: *Writer Nathaniel Gadsden, leads a weekly writers' group at the MetroArts Center on Forster Street. Gadsden is also director of Harrisburg Community Ministries, Tressler Lutheran Services.*

BELOW: *Making a "front porch playground," the Susquehanna River flows by the city on its western side. This aerial view is taken from Uptown looking south.* ABOVE: *The Harrisburg Symphony Barge Concert annually attracts thousands of listeners on boats and at Riverfront Park.* ABOVE LEFT: *Originating on City Island, horse-drawn carriage rides travel across the Walnut Street bridge to important sites in Center City including the Capitol.*

HANOVER PUBLIC
LIBRARY
HANOVER, PA.

PREVIOUS PAGE: *City Island's picturesque setting is home to professional baseball and football, park eateries, shops, miniature golf, boating marinas, playgrounds, pavilions, a train and other attractions.*
RIGHT: *Late evening sun reflects on the railroad bridge piers spanning the river.*
BELOW: *The riverfront is active with strollers, spectators, festival attractions, and leisure boaters at numerous warm-weather events.*

TOP: *The Pride of the Susquehanna, a paddle wheeler, offers dinner, special event and regularly scheduled cruises during the summer.* LEFT: *During the winter holidays, City Island glows with lights and decor of the season as well as activities for all ages.* ABOVE: *The inflated trampoline is a favorite attraction along the riverfront during Kipona days.*

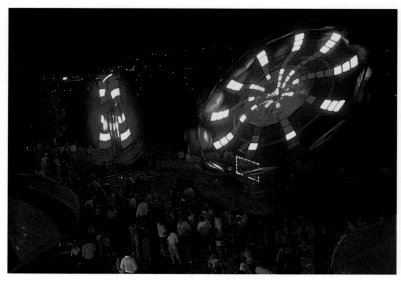

ABOVE: *Viewing the Susquehanna River and city from Wormleysburg or Negley Park on the west shore at sunset or with evening lights reflecting on the water is any romantic's delight.* LEFT: *Amusement rides attract children to weekend events on the riverfront.*

BOTTOM: *Evening light shines through the arches of the Conrail Bridge forming a border to the skyline viewed from the I-83 bridge.* **BELOW:** *The Conrail Bridge is reflected in the river in the stillness of early morning.* **RIGHT:** *A fisherman enjoys the coolness of the Susquehanna's water within view of the Capitol's dome on a hot summer afternoon.*

Built by the founder of Harrisburg, John Harris, Jr., the John Harris-Simon Cameron Mansion, 219 S. Front Street, later became the home of President Lincoln's Secretary of War and U.S. Senator, Simon Cameron. It is now a museum and home of the Historical Society of Dauphin Co. **ABOVE:** *The Mansion's drawing room has a silver urn and Bavarian etched color glass windows.* **TOP RIGHT:** *Built in 1766, the Mansion has incurred additions (southeast side).* **FAR RIGHT:** *A portrait of Mrs. James Cameron hangs in the library.* **RIGHT:** *The local limestone house museum is listed on the National Register of Historic Places (northside).*

Chapter 2

Harrisburg's Architecture

By David J. Morrison

David Morrison is executive director of the American Institute of Architects, Pennsylvania

I like to think that a city's most important exhibit is its architecture. It's on display, free of charge, 24 hours a day. It conveys the most enduring message about who we are, where we came from and, most importantly, where we're headed.

Our buildings, our skyline, and our streetscapes express a primary civic message that isn't easily "spin-doctored" into something it isn't. What you see is what you get. Day in and day out. Photography tells the truth. A sidewalk stroll exposes a vivid reality that either is good or bad, pleasant or unpleasant, hospitable or hostile. Important? You bet!

The outward appearance of our buildings is like the clothes we wear in public. Only, just imagine having to select a suit of clothes you'll have to wear for the next few decades! What do they say about you? How do you function in them? Are you comfortable in them? How will you be judged?

Architecture, like clothing, isn't merely about appearance. Having durability and value is important. And let's be sure we have inner layers that work, comfortably, keeping us warm in winter and cool in summer.

Harrisburg, in my view, has a nice, classic wardrobe. Not trendy. Not dated. It suits us. It's a strong, sensible architectural wardrobe that's been developed over several centuries. We're especially lucky in some regards. Our architecture and our city have the special benefit of a beautiful setting, framed by purple mountains and reflected in the waters of one of America's most magnificent rivers.

We're fortunate, also, that Harrisburg's architectural wardrobe currently enjoys enlightened professional supervision. For the last two decades, Mayor Steve Reed has functioned, you might say, as our civic haberdasher, assembling a fully updated look that mixes bold new elements with old favorites that are back in style. It's a look that bears his signature. I'm one who's had the privilege of occasionally holding the other end of the tape measure or pointing out a loose button. I'm part of a citizenry that today feels architecturally well-dressesd!

The defining elements of Harrisburg's appearance are its two most enduring features: the Pennsylvania State Capitol and the Susquehanna riverfront. Each alone is a powerful visage. Together, they create an urban trademark that is unique in America.

Harrisburg's riverfront combines a natural beauty that is millions of years old with a manmade environment shaped over the past quarter-millennium. In 1719, John Harris chose this location for business purposes (transportation and commerce) and his son, John Harris, Jr., established a town and envisioned its

potential as an important American city. Though his goal of attracting the U.S. Capital here was not achieved, the Harris family did succeed in attracting the capital of America's most important state in 1810.

The Harris and Maclay mansions, both built in the 18th century, established the riverfront as the residential location of choice. Midway between them, Robert Harris of the third generation built the town's first upscale real estate development, employing no less than the architect of the Capitol, Stephen Hills. Not unexpectedly, his project came to be known as "Governors' Row."

From then until the Great Depression, Harrisburg's social and business leaders continued to build and occupy stately Front Street mansions facing the Susquehanna. Much remains of the fabric of this legendary streetscape, whose lifestyle is immortalized in John O'Hara's novel A Rage to Live. O'Hara's "Fort Penn" of mid-century is today's "Llanview" referenced in the television soap opera "One Life to Live."

A coincidence of geography ensured the beautification of the riverfront in the 19th century, but a concerted campaign of civic activism saved it in the 20th. In the 1820s, the Pennsylvania Canal was routed 12 blocks east of Front Street, near present-day Cameron Street, following the low elevation of the Paxton Creek. As a result, railroads, factories, and warehouses were concentrated there, not along the river as in many other river towns. A century later, it was the "City Beautiful Movement" that transformed the river's edge from a garbage dump and sewer outlet into Riverfront Park, whose renaissance we enjoy today.

Astute urban planning in the 20th century has, for the most part, preserved the foreground of the State Capitol from high-rise obstructions. Its magnificent dome, rising 272 feet from its elevated founda-

tion on Capitol Hill, remains a prominent, if not dominant, feature of the skyline from many directions. Elegant State Street, from the Capitol steps to Kunkel Plaza two blocks west, strives to retain its purpose as a dramatic vista connecting the river and the home of the world's oldest democracy.

Harrisburg is a city of neighborhoods, spreading north, east, and south. South Harrisburg, containing some of the earliest remnants of the city's past, includes the quaint working-class housing of "Shipoke," now one of the most fashionable neighborhoods in central Pennsylvania. Its river views, its rich mix of ante-bellum and Victorian architecture, and its strong neighborhood identity create a truly satisfying living environment.

Historic streetscapes remain intact through

PAGES 28 AND 29: *With a $9.5 million restoration completed in 1998, the Sylvan Heights mansion built in 1866 by Col. John Brandt, is now The YWCA of Greater Harrisburg John Crain Kunkel Center for Women and Children.*
FAR LEFT: *The Broad Street Market is the oldest continuously operated market house in Pennsylvania.* **LEFT:** *Established in 1860, The Market has benefited from restorations beginning in 1976.* **RIGHT:** *the Salem Reformed Church, 231 Chestnut St., was built in 1822.*

much of Harrisburg. The march of time -and the corresponding changes in residential architectural styles - can be seen as one progresses north: the Civil War-era and late 19th century houses of the Capitol Area neighborhood and Midtown; the turn-of-the-century blocks of turreted townhouses that are remarkably unchanged in Old Uptown; and the early 20th century twins and singles of New Uptown, whose lawns, driveways, and suburban elbow-room accompanied the advent of streetcars and personal automobiles.

To the east, along the prominent arteries of State, Market, and Derry streets, stand such old neighborhoods as Schreinertown, Summit Terrace, Allison Hill, and Mount Pleasant. Built adjoining the vast employment opportunities along the railroad corridor and its spurs (not to mention the significant job market once provided by the railroad industry itself), this tapestry of neighborhoods enjoys the geographic advantage of the high bluffs overlooking downtown Harrisburg and the Capitol.

Ours is a downtown of tall buildings and distinctive architecture that respectfully adjoins a still-visible Capitol dome. The erection of the new Capitol in 1906 unleashed an upgrading of the city's architecture that began with "Harrisburg's first skyscraper," an eight-story office building that remains the northwest cornerstone of Market Square. Its companions today on Market Square are the office towers and Hilton Hotel, whose governmental contemporary, by no coincidence, is the Capitol's acclaimed East Wing addition, completed in 1986. Great eras in state government and great eras in the life of Harrisburg have gone hand-in-hand since 1810.

Entering a new millennium and the fourth century of John Harris' colonial outpost at the riverside crossroads of two important Indian trails, Harrisburg today enjoys the best of its accumulated heritage. We've endured and thrived as a national crossroad of river, rail, and highway transportation. We've evolved as a city of inviting architecture and unusually commodious public places.

We remain the seat of a citadel of democracy, the present-day home of William Penn's "Holy

Experiment," the radical 17th century notion of equality and acceptance that has since become the model and ideal for governments everywhere.

At the turn of the third millennium, Harrisburg is, as much as ever, a "City Beautiful." We've worked hard to make it so and to keep it so.

LEFT: *The State Arsenal, N. 18th and Herr Sts. was erected in 1874 and rebuilt in 1914.* **ABOVE:** *The William Maclay Mansion, a Georgian-styled structure at 401 N. Front St. was built in 1791.* **RIGHT:** *Author David J. Morrison chats with Steve Neiman, CEO of Neiman Group Advertising at the newly restored Harrisburg Transportation Center lobby in the early 90s, soon after its restoration. The Neiman Group has offices in the Center.*

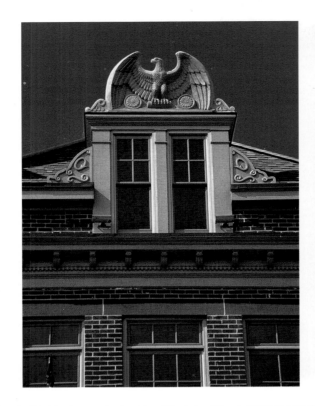

TOP LEFT: *The Fire Museum of Greater Harrisburg, 1820 N. 4th St., holds a large collection of antique fire apparatus, including this 1935 Mack 75' aerial truck.* ABOVE: *Originally dedicated in 1899 as the Reily Hose Co. No. 10., the firehouse was restored in 1995. Left: A life-size diorama at the museum displays an 1894 hose wagon and an 1850 hose carriage.* TOP FAR LEFT: *The 3rd floor dormer illustrates the Victorian style of the firehouse.*

RIGHT: *Now renovated as the Old City Hall distinctive apartments, the building at 423 Walnut St. was built as a school and then became the city's municipal building.* **FAR RIGHT:** *The YMCA at N. Front and North Sts. uses Moorish motifs in its doorway tile accents.* **BELOW FAR RIGHT:** *Now the Belco Credit Union, 401-403 N. 2nd St., the classic Queen-Anne Victorian mansion was built in 1887.* **BELOW CENTER:** *The First United Methodist Church at Boas and Susquehanna Sts. is one of Harrisburg's many historic churches.* **BELOW:** *Built in 1884 as The Pennsylvania Railroad Station, the Harrisburg Transportation Center was beautifully restored in 1985.*

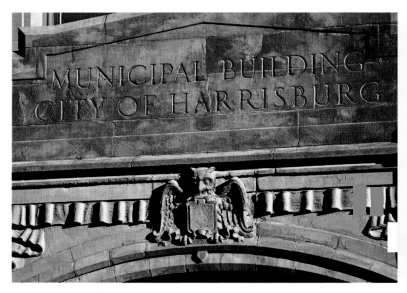

37

ABOVE: *The last remaining cast iron storefront in the city, dated c.1868, is located at 236 North St.* ABOVE RIGHT: *This single family mansion built in 1904 at 333 South 13th St. is now the Discipleship Center.* FAR RIGHT: *Located on a complete block of restored Front St. mansions, the Simonton Mansion, 317 N. Front St., was built about 1860.* RIGHT: *The spire of historic Zion Lutheran Church, 15 S. 4th St., rises against the modern Rachel Carson State Office Building at 400 Market St.*

The James Donald Cameron Mansion at 407 N. Front St. was built in second empire- style in 1863. U.S. Senator, James Donald was the son of U.S. Senator Simon Cameron, both prominent Harrisburg figures. St. Patrick's Cathedral chapel is in the background.

BOTTOM: *Built in 1927, the King Mansion with its wide portico, indoor swimming pool, and Italianate features, was the largest single family home in the city. The mansion at 2201 N. Front St. is now the Merchants and Businessmen's Mutual Insurance building.*
BELOW: *Once a family mansion, 2501 N. Front St. is now occupied by the Harrisburg Builders Exchange.*

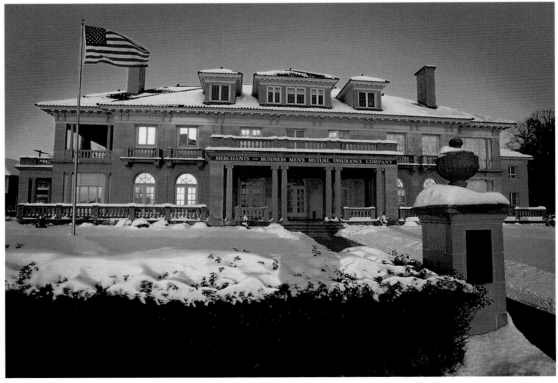

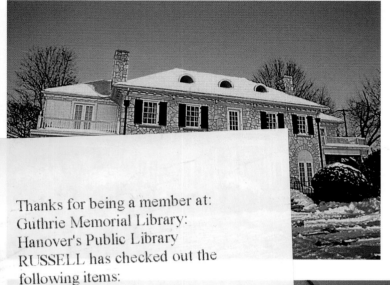

Thanks for being a member at:
Guthrie Memorial Library:
Hanover's Public Library
RUSSELL has checked out the
following items:

1. Harrisburg : renaissance of a
   capital city
   Barcode: 34007000844659
   Due: 2018-03-12 11:59 PM
2. Reindeer games
   Barcode: 34007000885751
   Due: 2018-02-26 11:59 PM
3. The walking dead The
   complete seventh season
   Barcode: 34007002291479
   Due: 2018-02-26 11:59 PM

02/19/18
717-632-5183
www.yorklibraries.org

LEFT: *This mansion at 2601 N. Front St., now occupied by Skelly and Loy, Inc, was built during the 1920's heyday of opulent Front St. homes.* **BELOW:** *Spring blossoms adorn Front and Market Sts. at the Keystone Plaza (left) completed in 1992. The Penn National Insurance building on Market Square designed by Harrisburg architect Martin Murray and completed in 1997 rises above the Dauphin Co. Veterans Memorial Office building at 112 Market St.*

RIGHT: *The statue of Pennsylvania Governor Andrew Curtin stands in the center of Camp Curtin Park at N. 6th and Woodbine Sts. The Park commemorates Harrisburg's strategic Civil War location.*
FAR RIGHT: *Youth participate in the Memorial Day parade along N. 6th St.*
BELOW: *Dressed in Civil War period costume, women stroll in the Uptown Memorial Day parade.*

ABOVE: *The 1814 Federal-period Fort Hunter Mansion is located just north of Harrisburg on a 35-acre site along the Susquehanna River.* TOP RIGHT: *A Victorian-style water basin sits in a Mansion bedroom.* RIGHT: *The Fort Hunter Mansion and Park includes an icehouse, a tavern, a blacksmith shop and the historic barn, renovated with modern facilities for programs and meetings.*

LEFT: *Four double houses in Shipoke, often referred to as Pancake Row, were built by Alfred Pancake of all wood in 1889. The homes are restored in bright Victorian colors.* BOTTOM: *The 19th century townhouses in the 301 block of N. 2nd St. retain their original appearance while serving as offices.* BELOW: *The City exhibits many architectural styles including the briefly popular Spanish colonial revival of the 1920s displayed in the Valencia Apartments at 2800 N. 2nd St.*

THIS PAGE BOTTOM: *The twin houses at 800-810 N. 16th St. are early 20th century English Tudor, those to the right retaining the exposed half-timber construction.* **BELOW LEFT:** *The Civic Club, originally the Fleming Mansion built in 1902, is an excellent example of English Tudor Revival-style.* **BELOW RIGHT:** *Capitol neighborhood buildings retain their 1900 residential character.*

ABOVE and **LEFT:** *Entire blocks of richly detailed Victorian-style homes built during a rapid growth period between the Civil War and WWI remain intact on Allison Hill (top: 23-29 S. 17th St. and bottom: 129-141 N. 13th St.).*

RIGHT: *The Forum Building of neoclassic design, constructed of Indiana limestone on a base of Massachusetts granite is richly decorated. The exterior sculptures depict themes from history, literature and art.* BELOW: *Artists working with architect Arnold W. Brunner completed decorating the 472' X 200' building in 1931. Designed to complement the Capitol, the Forum Building houses a concert hall, the state library and Commonwealth offices.*

LEFT: *Located on the Capitol grounds, an equestrian statue commemorates John Frederick Hartranft (1830-1889) who earned the Medal of Honor of Valor at the 1st battle of Bull Run.* BELOW FAR LEFT AND FAR RIGHT: *The City of Harrisburg Volunteer Firemen's World War I memorial lists firemen killed in service. It stands at Verbeke St. in Riverfront Park.* BELOW LEFT: *The bronze statue in Riverfront Park at Cumberland St. also recalls WWI soldiers killed.* BELOW: *The Mexican-American War memorial stands to the south of the Capitol Annex.*

Chapter 3

Harrisburg's Parks and Gardens

by Tina Manoogian-King

Tina Manoogian-King is Director of Parks and Recreation for the City of Harrisburg

That history repeats itself is easily seen when exploring Harrisburg's parks, where the vision of Mayor Stephen R. Reed's Parks Improvement Program has expanded and restored grandeur to the region's largest recreational facilities.

To appreciate the recent years' accomplishments, we must first realize that, as the twentieth century opened, few parks existed and little thought had been given to preserving open spaces for future recreational use. That all changed in 1901 as students and proponents of the renowned Frederick Olmstead, designer of New York City's Central Park, returned to Harrisburg with a definite vision for their hometown's future.

LEFT: *The growth of redbud trees illustrates the fine gardens on the campus of the Harrisburg Area Community College.* **BELOW:** *A biker enjoys springtime in Riverfront Park.*

J. Horace McFarland and Mira Lloyd Dock sparked establishment of the Harrisburg League for Municipal Improvements, an energetic civic organization that focused on improving and enhancing Harrisburg's parks and open spaces. From their efforts, sometimes referred to as the "City Beautiful Movement," came the city's first official parks system and its expansion in the next decade to include Riverfront Park, Reservoir Park, City Island, and what is known today as the Capital Area Greenbelt. In ensuing decades, additional facilities established included Italian Lake Park, Sunshine Park, and the park at Seventh and Radnor Streets.

This dynamic municipal improvement effort was a result of the belief of society at the turn of the century that enhancing the quality of life of a community's citizens was as important as ensuring good wages and safe working conditions. With assistance and support from top civic, political, and professional leaders, Harrisburg's fledgling park system quickly became a magnet for residents and visitors. The beautiful settings of Riverfront Park and what was then known as Island Park quickly became regional attractions that hosted thousands daily. Sunday strolls in Riverfront Park became an after-church ritual for the region's middle and upper classes, while thousands more thrilled to athletic feats of such greats as Jim Thorpe, Babe Ruth, and Satchel Paige at Island Park's professional ballfield.

By the end of World War I, the City Beautiful Movement had slowed; only a handful of new parks and playgrounds were added to the system between 1920 and the early 1960s.

As the city's population and regional esteem began to decline after the U.S. Supreme Court school desegregation decision in 1954, so, too, the parks began to suffer. With no capital budget and shrinking maintenance budgets, the city's emerald jewels were virtually abandoned by the early 1960s. But the civil unrest of the mid-'60s, sparked in part by the assassination of civil rights leader Rev. Dr. Martin Luther King, Jr., was catalyst for the next stage of development in the parks system.

Responding to escalating racial tensions across the country, the federal government poured billions of dollars into America's cities, creating new employment and recreational opportunities for minorities and the disenfranchised. Harrisburg's portion of this largess resulted in its first-ever community swimming pools, on North Sixth Street and South Eighteenth Street, and addition of 19 new neighborhood playgrounds.

The renewed interest and attention was short-lived, however, and by the early '70s, the parks system once again had deteriorated into disrepair and blight. The situation was made even worse by 1972's devastating Tropical Storm Agnes flood that left in its wake a city that was a shadow of its former self.

By the early 1980s, Harrisburg's once grand parks system mirrored the blighted city around it. City Island, largely overgrown, neglected, and unused for decades, was a haven for nefarious behavior, and city playgrounds were used more for open air drug markets than for recreation. Near bankruptcy and declared the second-most-distressed city in the nation, Harrisburg barely had enough funds for police salaries, let alone staff to maintain the parks system.

In 1982 reformist mayor Stephen R. Reed was elected; and a proverbial Phoenix was about to rise from the ashes of neglect. Paying homage to the earlier City Beautiful Movement, Reed knew that if Harrisburg was to once again become a viable place to live, work, and play, its entertainment and recreational opportunities had to become something that every resident and visitor could take pride in. His vision led to establishment of the Mayor's Parks Improvement Program in 1983 and creation of the

LEFT: *Beautifully crafted signs welcome visitors at the Walnut St. entrance to Reservoir Park.* ABOVE: *The memorial to Rose Roy (1936-1998) is located in Riverfront Park at Seneca St. Rose was an avid, committed volunteer for many City organizations.*

city's Special Events Office in 1984. The results of these two initiatives are evident throughout Harrisburg today.

At the center of the Parks Improvement Program was total rehabilitation of nearly all the parks, playgrounds, and pools. Since 1984, the city has invested more than $28 million in 22 of the city's 27 parks and playgrounds. Leading this wave of municipal attention has been the breathtaking transformation of City Island into one of the nation's most beautiful and popular waterfront destinations.

The "bricks and mortar" effort was matched by creation of recreational and entertainment events and activities, ranging from small neighborhood block parties to major regional events drawing hundreds of thousands of visitors. With more than 200 events annually, this cornucopia of fun today draws nearly 2 million people a year. Thousands more daily use and enjoy the more than two dozen parks, playgrounds, and open spaces throughout the city.

Harrisburg's parks and open spaces, with its 450 acres at 27 different recreational sites, and the emerald ribbon of the Greenbelt snaking through an additional 1,200 acres of city and suburban green space,

are considered one of the finest municipal park systems in the state. Major new investment by Mayor Reed in human resources and other capital investment has allowed dramatic expansion in maintenance and program personnel.

Today, on the dawn of a new millennium, Harrisburg's grand park system surely exceeds even the wildest dreams of its founders. Their legacy indeed has become our own.

Some of the major elements realized from Mayor Reed's Improvement Program include:

Capital Area Greenbelt. Formerly known as the Harrisburg Bike Path, restoring and expanding the Greenbelt, a 1,200–acre emerald necklace became a priority in the Mayor's parks' program. The city's efforts have been spurred by the Capital Area Greenbelt Association, an ambitious citizens group (see Norman Lacasse's essay on page 70). To date, 14.6 miles of the 20.1-mile parkway have been restored, including extensive landscaping, pavement resurfacing, stream embankment stabilization, and installation of gates, signage, park benches, and information kiosks. Lighting and other amenities will be added in future phases.

Riverfront Park. A 4.5 mile-long ribbon of parkland along the city's western boundary, with an array of public art, Riverfront Park is regarded by many as

LEFT: *The sculpture,* Evolution *by Boris Blai, graces Reservoir Park.* RIGHT: *The Peace Garden, planned and maintained by the local chapter of the Physicians for Social Responsibility, abounds with flowers during the summer but has a winter respite.* BELOW: *Summer concerts at Italian Lake (the Dixieland Express plays) and Reservoir Park are anticipated by residents and visitors alike.*

the city's most-favored green space. Its linear design encourages activities ranging from relaxing strolls to weekly running races and the midstate's top holiday festivals. The 13 overlooks and 13 steps down to the river memorialize the 13 original colonies. Unique themed gardens such as Midtown's Sunken Garden and uptown's Peace Garden provide urban arboretums unlike anything else in the midstate. The newest additions include the Kunkel and Swenson Plazas at State and Walnut Streets respectively.

Reservoir Park. This 90-acre area, established in 1845, is the oldest and largest municipal park in south-central Pennsylvania, and was renovated in three phases. In 1992 came rehabilitation of the 1898 mansion and a nearby picnic pavilion, creation of a five-building artists' village, and restoration of the 1940s-era bandshell, roadway reconstruction and repaving, and installation of antique-style streetlights, new walkways, fountains, gardens, and plazas. In 1993 formal French and drift gardens, lighted walkways, public art, and outdoor seating were added. The 1995 third phase added additional gardens and walkways, an expanded children's playground, restoration of the historic Brownstone Building as an arts and education center, reconstruction of basketball and tennis courts and installation of a new

entranceway and park ranger station. Still to come is the new National Civil War Museum at the top of the park–the highest point in the city–expected to be completed by summer 2000.

City Island. What was a 63-acre weed-and-debris-filled sore on the soul of downtown for nearly three decades is now the focal point of the comprehensive Mayor's Waterfront Enhancement Program and one of central Pennsylvania's favorite recreational and entertainment destinations. The transformation began with construction of RiverSide Stadium in 1986 and now includes the Skyline Sports Complex, marinas, boat ramps, picnic pavilions, and gazebos, along with RiverSide Village Park, Harbourtown children's play area, the Water Golf miniature golf course, Island Railroad, and the Pride of the Susquehanna paddlewheel riverboat.

Italian Lake. Located uptown, this exquisite 9.5-acre park recently was restored to its mid-century grandeur. Restoration work included dredging the entire lake, installation of new walkways, lighting, landscaping, gardens, signage, and the construction of the first retaining walls along the lake's northern pool. Its newest garden is dedicated to the late Rev. Clyde Roach, a beloved and respected pastor in the city. *H*

RIGHT: *Located near Woodbine St. in the Peace Garden within Riverfront Park, one of three sculptures by world-renowned artist, Dr. Frederick Franck, is the "Unkillable Human," a replica of a shadow burned into concrete when the atomic bomb struck Hiroshima.*
FAR RIGHT: *Enjoying the springtime beauty, A runner jogs along the southern end of the more than four-mile long Riverfront Park.*
BELOW: *Framed by the rich colors of the spring cherry blossoms, residents stroll along an Uptown stretch of Riverfront Park.*

RIGHT: *The Midtown's mix of early spring blossoms with the rebirth of sycamore tree leaves gives splendor to Riverfront Park.* **FAR RIGHT:** *Benches and gardens along the Park provide quiet places for resting and watching the river and sunsets.* **BELOW:** *Through the joint effort of the City and Riverfront Peoples Park, a nonprofit volunteer group, Sunken Gardens, located between Cumberland and Verbeke Sts., has been restored, earning Historic Harrisburg Association's preservation award. The southern end of the gardens are shown here.*

PREVIOUS PAGE: *The Shakespeare Festival performs* Taming of the Shrew *at sunset. The band shell at Reservoir Park, 18th and Walnut Sts., is the venue for numerous events from April through October. The City's recent restoration and additions to the park include: the Mansion (right) and surrounding grounds; FAR RIGHT: gardens, walkways and sculptures; and BELOW: a children's playground. Originally designed by noted Boston landscape architect, Warren Manning, beginning in the 1890's, much of the recent work has been performed by H. Edward Black's Harrisburg firm.*

RINGING THE CITY WITH GREEN

by Norman Lacasse

Norman Lacasse is the immediate past president of the Capital Area Greenbelt Association

On December 20, 1900, Mira Lloyd Dock delivered a speech on the "City Beautiful" to the Harrisburg Board of Trade. At that time, Harrisburg was not a nice place in which to live—streets were unpaved, there were many factories and mills that emitted fumes and polluted the air, and the river bank was where residents dumped their trash and coal ashes, since the city didn't provide any collection service. Sewer lines emptied directly on the east shore of the Susquehanna and the city pumped water—unfiltered and untreated—directly into residents' taps. Typhoid was rampant.

Just back from a forestry tour in Europe, Dock showed the group lantern slides of what European cities had done with their parks and streets. The contrast between Europe and Harrisburg was great, and Dock's public speaking skills electrified the audience. Soon, seven men were appointed to a Harrisburg Improvement Committee to chart a course to improve the city's living conditions. They hired three experts to recommend improvements in sanitation, street paving, and city parks.

Boston landscape architect Warren Manning, the consultant for parks, recommended a parked river front, expansion of the existing Reservoir Park, creation of a landscaped park at Wetzel's Swamp north of the city (now known as Wildwood Lake Park), and a ring boulevard encircling the city to connect its parks. On February 18, 1902, the voters approved a bond issue to fund the improvements by a 2-1 vote.

Over the next 15 years, supported by three additional bond issues, extensive improvements were made. Park acreage increased from 46 in 1902 to 958 by 1915. The riverfront was cleaned up with installation of a sewer interceptor covered with a broad walkway.

ABOVE: *The Greenbelt sign appears frequently along the 20-mile biking and walking trail.* **LEFT:** *Jess Hayden, an outdoor enthusiast, discusses nature with her children at Wildwood Park, a Dauphin Co. wildlife sanctuary which includes an education center. The Greenbelt embraces the northern end of Wildwood.*

Concrete steps were built for three miles to prevent erosion of the riverbank. The ring boulevard grew rapidly at first with completion of Wildwood Lake Park, Riverfront Park, and the two-mile Cameron Parkway along Spring Creek at the southern border of the city. The Paxtang Parkway was the next section built, connecting the greenway to Reservoir Park. Unfortunately, the section from Reservoir Park to Wildwood Lake was never completed.

There are several reasons why the 20–mile parkway was never completed, chief among them the effects of the post–World War II migration of city residents to the suburbs. City dwellers who had enjoyed Sunday picnics in their favorite city park now were at backyard barbecues. The exodus devastated city budgets; recreational amenities are generally the first casualty. The Harrisburg parkway eventually was gated and abandoned, and nature moved quickly to reclaim the land.

The Capital Area Greenbelt Association was formed in 1990 to restore the completed sections of the greenway and complete what hadn't been done. In the past 10 years it has accomplished much with volunteer help from the community, supported by various groups, grants, and donated materials and equipment. Significant grants obtained in 1999 will allow the 20-mile loop to be essentially completed in the next two years.

There were times in the past decade when it seemed that maintaining such an extensive linear park with volunteers was not possible. The turning point may have been a confrontation with McDonald's and the county over proposed siting of a fast food restaurant on the greenbelt. Almost overnight, the greenbelt became an accepted institution and a household word.

The completion of additional sections, addition of the Five Senses Garden, and much hard work by many individuals and groups has resulted in greatly increased usage of the greenbelt. There's now no doubt that the Capital Area Greenbelt is and forever will be one of the gems of our Capital City.

The Greenbelt Association works regularly on Saturdays to upgrade the beltway. Norm Lacasse (2nd from left) and Glenn Grimm (1st from left) install a gateway along the trail's northern-stretch with assistance from youth from several youth groups. BELOW: Riding along Spring Creek, young cyclists enjoy the Cameron Parkway section of the Greenbelt.

Residents in the neighborhoods near Italian Lake at N. 3rd and Division Sts., enjoy the Park's year round beauty as the seasons change. A few of Harrisburg's most elegant homes, reflected in the lake in early spring (left) and in the winter (below) line the Park's west side. The Park, a swamp reclaimed in the 1930's, has a Japanese bridge often used as a background for wedding photography and a water fountain bronze sculpture of three dancing nudes created by Giuseppe Donato named, "Dance of the Eternal Spring".

HANOVER PUBLIC
LIBRARY
HANOVER, PA.

PREVIOUS PAGE: *Italian Lake occupies 9 acres including several acres of Italian Renaissance-style gardens, walkways, lawns and an outdoor stage. Springtime is gloriously beautiful in many areas of residential Harrisburg.* ABOVE LEFT: *The Pennsylvania Bar Association, 111-115 State St.;* ABOVE MIDDLE: *Division and 3rd Sts. at the Zembo Temple;* ABOVE RIGHT: *2700 block of N. Front Street;* RIGHT: *magnolias in Bellevue Park, Harrisburg's planned residential community of mansions, winding lanes and woodlands;* BELOW: *Chestnut and 21st Sts.*

Chapter 4

Whitaker Center – Harrisburg's Crown Jewel Bringing Renewed Life Downtown

by John Hope

John Hope is a Harrisburg freelance writer

A change has come to Harrisburg's downtown that is as significant as the turn-of-the-century City Beautiful Movement.

For at least two decades, it's been said that Harrisburg rolls up its downtown sidewalks at night. It wasn't always that way. When there were no malls, downtown was the place to go for entertainment and shopping. Once, there were four splendid movie palaces. And two department stores, three 5-and-10s, and many specialty stores welcomed busy shoppers.

But over the past 30 years, Harrisburg's nightlife has given way to suburban malls with their multi-screen cinema complexes and great variety of stores, aided by ample free parking. While there have been cultural programs at the Forum and Market Square Presbyterian Church, night sporting events on City Island, and a surge of new restaurants, by and large Harrisburg's downtown lives and dies between 11 a.m. and 2 p.m. Until now.

As far back as the early 1970s, there was talk that Harrisburg should follow the lead of other cities and build a performing arts venue to attract people downtown at night. But none of those proposals succeeded. We waited to pull all the necessary forces together to do it right–and to do it in a way that hasn't been tried anywhere else in the world! Enter the Whitaker Center for Science and the Arts.

Everyone who has walked or driven past the Whitaker Center construction at Third and Market streets has formed an opinion of the project based on its exterior appearance; some love it and some hate it. For the architect, the building was an opportunity to research the history of Market Street and create a design evoking images of that past history while also blending with the contemporary scene. Use of the sandstone and slate color scheme was part of the attempt to honor the past.

But the varying opinions about the building's appearance can't detract from the programming fea-
tures that set it apart from any other place in the country. What makes the Whitaker Center unique is its deliberate integration of science and the performing arts. Recognizing that many people can be intimidated by science, the Whitaker Center uses art to explain science and draw people to learn in new and interesting ways. And it uses science to explain art. The result is a center that appeals to all ages and is a bridge between daytime and nighttime excitement downtown.

What led to the Whitaker Center's success when so many other proposals had failed was its ability to bring together government and the private and non-profit sectors in a concerted effort to make the dream a reality.

Mayor Stephen R. Reed and City Council were totally behind the project and provided $6 million. The city obtained a grant of $21 million from state government. When the Whitaker Foundation was looking for a project worthy to bear its name to honor AMP, Inc. founder Uncas A. Whitaker and his wife Helen, they did not need to look any further than the proposed science and arts center. The foundation's gift of more than $8 million helped the fundraising considerably, as did a donation of $1.5 million from AMP and significant sums from other corporations and foundations.

With adequate funds available, the center's leadership could attract talented and experienced staff from around the country to this exciting, unique undertaking. The result is an interactive science center, an IMAX theater, and a state-of-the-art performance hall.

The Science Center has more than 200 interactive exhibits to interest and instruct young and old alike. Nine permanent exhibits examine different aspects of the relationship between science and the arts–The Gateway, Health and Wellness, Gallery of Mathematics in Nature and Art Mathematics, People

and Diversity, Environment and Ecology, Forces and Motion, Sound and Music, Color and Light, and Kids' Hall. Two flagship exhibits linking science and the arts are "Bodies in Motion: The Physics of Dance" and "Backstage Science: The Physics of Theater."

Operating both day and night on a more ambitious performance schedule than that of any other IMAX operation will be the Grass/Rite Aid IMAX Theater, a 200-seat theater with a movie screen six-stories high.

The other Whitaker Center element that will again bring people downtown at night is the 664-seat Sunoco Performance Theater. Every patron is assured a clear view of the stage and no one is seated more than 65 feet from it.

Looking back on all that has happened to make the Whitaker Center a reality, Mayor Stephen R. Reed says it is "an unprecedented and historic means of expressing and supporting this city's and region's creativity and excellence in the arts, cultural pursuits,

PREVIOUS PAGE: *The Sunoco Performance Theater includes 14 theater boxes and will feature the finest in theater, dance and music.* **ABOVE:** *The Kunkel Gallery will be the venue for special events.* **RIGHT:** *The Whitaker Center is linked by walkways to the Hilton Hotel (l) and Strawberry Square (r).*

and education. As a first-of-its-kind facility in the nation that marries the arts and science, it is our portal to the rest of the world in saying that this is a dynamic and attractive place where you should want to live, work, and visit. Whitaker represents a never-before-seen partnership of the private, public, and non-profit sectors in this region which sets both a standard and an example for how we can do extraordinary, visionary, bold, and exciting things, as a region, in the 21st century." *H*

BELOW: *Artistic Director Marcia Dale Weary (left) refines the steps of the Central Pennsylvania Youth Ballet (CPYB) at a Rose Lehrman Arts Center dress rehearal. The school and performing company, which has achieved international recognition is the resident dance group at the Whitaker Center. BOTTOM: CPYB dancers Dipal Chatterjee, Ashley Bouder and George Banning perform* Delibes Variations *choreographed by Sherry Moray.*

BELOW: *The Harrisburg Dance Ensemble, a pre-professional group of The Harrisburg Dance Conservatory, gives a premiere performance of* Dracula, *choreographed by Nana Badrena. Dancers are Luis Bravo as Dracula and Meghan Bailey as Mina. The Conservatory, a school of dance, has a faculty of celebrated performers and experienced instructors for ages 3 through adult.*

ABOVE RIGHT: *Modern dance movements are performed by the Née Danse Company during the Greater Harrisburg ArtsFest at Harrisburg Area Community College (HACC). A modern repertory company, Née Danse, founded in 1994 by Artistic Director Della M. Cowall, conducts classes at its 923 N. 3rd St. studio.* RIGHT: *The Harrisburg Dance Ensemble, under the artistic direction of Rosemary Battista, performs at HACC's Rose Lehrman Arts Center.*

TOP NEAR RIGHT: *The band, Commit No Violence, performs at one of the four outdoor concert venues at the Greater Harrisburg Artsfest.* TOP FAR RIGHT: *Drummers of Ngozi, Inc. accompany a demonstration of martial arts at the Artsfest.* BOTTOM FAR RIGHT: *Artsfest enthusiasts try on hats from Ossi, a NYC-based artist, one of 300 artists and craftspersons invited.* NEAR RIGHT MIDDLE: *The annual Artsfest, organized by the Greater Harrisburg Arts Council, includes a Kidsfest, film festival and wine tasting.* NEAR RIGHT BOTTOM: *Yohanna Assidean greets a visitor at the African Family Festival held at Reservoir Park each year.* BELOW: *African garb-maker Fatousall of New York displays her designs at the African fest of music, food, and art planned by Ngozi, Inc.*

RIGHT: *The Ngozi dance class led by Rafiyqa Muhammad practices at the Neighborhood Center.* BOTTOM: *Scottish dance rehearsal, led by Robert Davidson (center), is held at the Metro Arts Center, 123 Forster St.* BELOW: *Danzante, a Harrisburg Spanish dance and instruction company directed by Camille Erice, performs at Central Dauphin East High School.*

LEFT: *Children's book illustrator and sculptor, Stephen Fieser, works in his N. 2nd St. studio.* BELOW: *Visitors examine Tina Brewer's "Feel the Joy" art at the Reservoir Park Mansion show, "Quilts." Organized by the African-American Museum of Harrisburg, the exhibit also includes local artist Christine Johnson's work (left in photo).* BOTTOM: *Louis Charles Gatling, Jr., a self-taught artist who has exhibited at Harrisburg's MetroArts and Doshi galleries, paints in his home studio.*

ABOVE: *Executive Director of the Susquehanna Art Museum, Jonathan J. VanDyke, a '95-'96 post-graduate student at Scotland's University of Glasgow, poses in the gallery with art by (l to r) Louise Fishman, Raphael Soyer, Isabel Bishop, Joan Brown ("Woman and Dog with Chinese Rug") and Jane Freillicher. RIGHT: April Tichenor, a museum art educator, teaches a jewelry making class at the Susquehanna Art Museum classroom.*

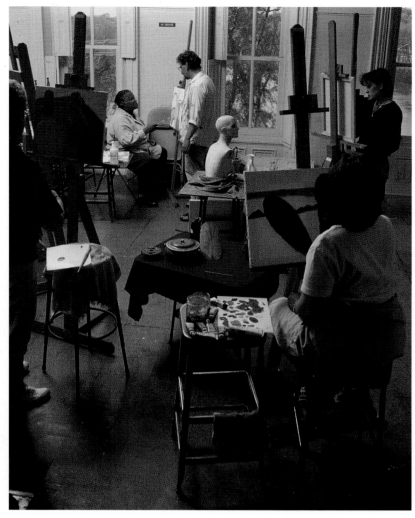

LEFT: *Art Association of Harrisburg (AAH) instructor Louis Rice teaches an art class at the 21 N. Front St. historic Gov. Findley Mansion, the home of AAH. Founded in 1926, AAH now mounts 36 exhibits annually at city locations and holds classes at the Jewish Community Center, Reservoir Park and other sites.*
BELOW: *Carrie Wissler-Thomas, President of AAH since 1986, examines Paul Nagle's sculpture, "Locotoon", at one of 10 annual shows at the AAH downtown mansion. Art in the background is by (l to r) Barbara Grant, Kimberly Berg, Dorothy Ricci and Alan Paulson.*

ABOVE: Sylvia Coslow (l), a supporter of the Art Association of Harrisburg (AAH), is hostess for one of the AAH informal meet-the-artist "Swinging Soirees" at her home. Rose Shuff (c), a copper-wire sculptor, has work sitting on the mantel and Nancy Mendes (r), a painter, displays her art on the wall.
ABOVE RIGHT: David F. Lenker, past president and teacher for over 20 years at AAH, poses at his Hummelstown gallery, Signature Artworks. A prolific watercolorist, his art includes many local scenes as well as work from his trips to Europe.
RIGHT: Ted Webber, a also respected Harrisburg watercolor artist, teaches still-life drawing techniques at the H. John Heinz Harrisburg Senior Center, 1824 North 4th St.

A Changing Visual Arts Collage

by Carrie Wissler-Thomas

Carrie Wissler-Thomas is president/executive director of the Art Association of Harrisburg

Born and raised in the little Lancaster County town of Ephrata, and armed with a fine arts degree from Hood College, I arrived in Harrisburg when Scott and I were married in 1972. One of my first actions after getting settled was to look up the Art Association of Harrisburg. I called, hoping for opportunities to exhibit my paintings, and ended up joining and being invited to volunteer as a hostess at Sunday "teas."

And thus I became immersed in Harrisburg's arts scene. I quickly learned that although it was "light years" away from the covered bridge, Amish-scene art of Ephrata, Harrisburg was nonetheless largely a watercolor-landscape town. Nick Ruggieri and his students reigned supreme in member exhibitions at the Art Association, and my "earth mother" nudes were not quite the thing in the shows. My fellow artists were a friendly, welcoming lot, however, and I soon got to know the important ones in town. The early '70s were the days when Bill Rohrbeck was painting and teaching, as were Vid Petrasic, Peg Brown, Karl Foster, Milford Patterson, Dave Lenker, and the Seven Lively Artists. Now, Bill, Milford, and Vid are gone, but Peg is still turning out fine watercolors. Karl is still teaching the AAH life class, and Dave the watercolor class, and the Seven Livelies number more than seven.

When I joined the Art Association, Mary Sheffer was in the midst of a seven-year stint as the board's energetic and forceful president. She was succeeded by Shim Lehrman, George Logan, Nancy Greenawalt, Peggy Berliner Ottens, Dave Lenker and, finally, me.

94

I'd come a long way since the days when I was told I poured tea well at Sunday receptions. And so had the art scene in Harrisburg.

In 1980, although watercolor landscapes still were popular, they were installed alongside expressionist pieces by Li Hidley and his students. The Doshi Gallery was showing cutting-edge contemporary art, and the Art Association had broken away from its conservative image.

Wanda Macomber wowed the public with her abstract-precisionist architectural paintings, as did Kathleen Piunti and Barbara Buer with their stunning photo-realism. Hidley and his students exhibited everywhere, with Charley Ann Rhoads, Bob Bissett, David Marcus, Pamela Wellington Lackey, and their fellow expressionists capturing prizes wherever they went. Betsy Staz, Noreen Boggs, and Erna Tunno all developed distinctive personal styles, and gained recognition as well. Susan Kogan (later Cohen) had founded "Women in the Arts," which ran each January at the then William Penn Museum and suddenly art by women was hot! Harrisburg was burgeoning as a real art center!

And the growth continued. When Gertrude Olmsted McCormick and her band of civic and social leaders founded the Art Association in 1926, it was the only visual arts game in town. By the time I was hired as Executive Director/President in the mid-'80s, AAH had been joined by Doshi, Tangerine Fine Arts, The People Place (later MetroArts), the Greater Harrisburg Arts Council and, on the west shore, Mechanicsburg Art Center and several fine commercial galleries. Juried shows were held everywhere, joining the oldest one begun by the Art Association in the late 1920s. The Greater Harrisburg Arts Festival began in 1962, and now ranks as one of the best in the country. Gallery Walk debuted in 1988 as a promotion of all of Harrisburg's fine art exhibition centers, and has been growing ever since.

Suddenly, businesses became more aware of the arts and their importance to the community. Allied Arts was founded and embarked on its first fund drive in 1986, with the Art Association the recipient of the first allocation check. The Association began attracting terrific business leaders like Charles Stoup and Morris Schwab to our board, which greatly enhanced our finances. As part of the trend for business to support the arts, AAH began a community exhibition program that now, in 1999, mounts 40 shows annually in ten area sites. Further evidence of area businesses' support for the arts is seen in the success of the AAH Sales Gallery. Since its inception in 1984, the Gallery has been the source of artwork for businesses such as PHICO, the Harrisburg Hilton and Towers, Corestates Bank, Penn National Insurance, Nationwide Insurance, and First Federal.

New artists have been moving to Harrisburg,

LEFT PAGE: *Charles "Li" Hidley, the Harrisburg master of expressionist painting and influential teacher, sits with a gallery of other artists' paintings of himself at his Midtown home. Moving to Harrisburg from New York City, Hidley started, encouraged and sustained a local group of expressionists. A prolific painter with over 1700 works of his own, he enjoys the art of his students and colleagues surrounding him: (l to r)* Country Boy *by Ruth Garonzik;* Contemplating *by Joseph Dudding;* Hidley *by Brian Rogers;* Time Flies *by Delores Kiely and* The Admiral *by Dr. Martin Plaut.* ABOVE: *Pottery instructor Jennifer Thompson and parent assistant Marty Elvin help students at the AAH Reservoir Park class.*

LEFT: *Business diners at the Hilton's upscale Golden Sheaf restaurant can enjoy a group of paintings by Barbara Bauer, a Harrisburg photo-realist. Placement of the art on the walls of the Golden Sheaf was arranged by the Art Association.* **BELOW:** *Don Lenker, an architect and painter, holds his watercolor of the John Harris Mansion which hangs with other works at the Harrisburg law offices of Metzger and Wickersham, 3211 N. Front St.*

attracted by the city's supportive ambiance. Our amazing Mayor Steve Reed has made Harrisburg an arts–friendly place. In 1991, under his guidance, Reservoir Park was completely revitalized with the caretaker's mansion renovated with gallery space for AAH and four studios built for AAH classes. The Art Association embarked on our summer "Art in the Park" program for youth in 1992, which has grown in popularity ever since. Art classes also are offered at Mechanicsburg's Art School and Galleries and at the Susquehanna Art Museum, which joined the Harrisburg scene in the 1990s to exhibit museum–calibre work from across the U.S.

The State Museum of Pennsylvania continues to mount excellent exhibitions of Pennsylvania artists' works, as well as the Art of the State, and the Governor's Residence hangs top–notch exhibits twice a year.

Now the Whitaker Center for Science and the Arts has opened. Although essentially a performance and science

venue, the Whitaker also includes an area for rotating visual arts exhibitions, installed by the area's major organizations. It, too, is part of the Harrisburg Gallery Walk.

The odyssey continues into the millennium. Harrisburg is a vibrant collage, with the lovely Susquehanna as the background for the colorful image. Eclectic and electric, the visual arts thrive in Harrisburg. *H*

*Right: Pamela deWall, direc-
tor of the Wednesday Club
Youth Chamber Orchestra,
teaches Suzuki violin to early
learners. BELOW: Student
Tielah Elizabeth Williams
practices violin.*

ABOVE NEAR RIGHT: *The Old World Folk Band, the widely traveled Harrisburg klezmer music group poses at the bank vaults of the Historic Harrisburg Association's historic bank lobby.* ABOVE FAR RIGHT: *The Susquehanna Folk Music Society which brings leading folk performers to the Harrisburg area, holds a Jamshop at the Fort Hunter Barn. Jamshops are gatherings of playing, singing and swapping songs.* RIGHT: *Steve Rudolph, resident jazz pianist at the Hilton Hotel and Towers, Market Sq., is also active in Central PA Friends of Jazz. CPFJ sponsors many educational jazz programs, encourages young artists and annually stages a festival which brings leading jazz musicians to a concert hall and many other city settings.*

FAR LEFT: *The Concertante Chamber Players, directed by Odin Rathnam, enjoy a group portrait in the Capitol Rotunda.* LEFT: *Harrisburg has birthed many choral groups including the Susquehanna Chorale, an award-winning chamber choral ensemble directed by Linda Tedford. The group performs here at the Market Square Presbyterian Church, also the venue for the Market Square Concerts.* BELOW: *The Harrisburg Singers, led by Susan Soloman Beckley, perform at the Forum.*

LEFT: *In the Harrisburg Opera Association's performance of Mozart's* The Abduction from the Seraglio *at Messiah College, Eric Dillner as Belmonte sings while Richard Crist as Osmin reads newspaper.*
LEFT BELOW: *Soprano Meagan Miller, who has performed with Opera Montreal and at the Merola Opera Center plays Constanze. Music Director for the production was Victoria Bond and Stage Director, Cynthia Edwards.* BELOW: *The Harrisburg Symphony Orchestra presents a concert at the Forum.* BELOW RIGHT: *The Harrisburg Choral Society provides an open sing-a-long night at the Pine St. Presbyterian Church.*

RIGHT: *Popcorn Hat Player, Ronald P. Zappile, is playing* Robin Hood, *but in a disguise costume.* FAR RIGHT: *At their theater in Strawberry Square, the Popcorn Hat Players, directed by J. Clark Nicholson, dramatize* Robin Hood *for school children. The Players also provide acting instruction and other drama-related services to schools.* BELOW: Taming of the Shrew *is performed at the annual outdoor Shakespeare Festival. Nicholson is also creative director for the Festival.*

PAGES 106-107: *Under the artistic direction of Donald Alsedek, Open Stage, a theater resident in downtown Harrisburg founded in 1983, performs* When She Danced *by Martin Sherman which dramatizes the life of Isadora Duncan.* **LEFT AND BELOW:** *The Theatre Harrisburg (TH) stages* Man of La Mancha *directed by Thomas Hostetter. Lead roles were played by Cary Burkett (Don Quixote) and Mary Smetak (Aldonza). Founded in 1926, TH is resident in the Whitaker Center for Science and the Arts.*

110

THE NEIGHBORHOODS
Chapter 5

Living in Community
by David B. Schwartz

David B. Schwartz, Ph.D., practices psychotherapy and writes books in his Midtown neighborhood

It wasn't the sound of the fire trucks racing up Second Street in the middle of the night that woke me; rather, it was the fact that I became aware they had stopped nearby. As I swung my feet to the floor, there was the sound of crackling radios and shouting voices. I hurriedly pulled on clothes and ran out of the house.

Fire trucks surrounded the old man's corner house. He stood on the sidewalk looking bewildered, clutching his ancient dog, as firefighters in helmets

LEFT: *Abundant produce is available Thursday through Saturday at the Hoover stand and many others at Midtown's Broad Street Market, a frequent meeting place for Harrisburg neighbors.* **ABOVE:** *The Reel St. block party is a chance for city police Officer Weaver-Carter to be a good neighbor.*

and air packs raced in and out of the house. They were the first people I'd ever seen go into the old man's house. He was a familiar sight in the neighborhood, shuffling along in his bedroom slippers as he walked the dog. He spoke to no one. When I mumbled a greeting as I passed him on his outings, he never looked up or even appeared to hear. He seemed as alone and isolated as a man could be, even in the heart of a city.

But tonight he was not alone, for dozens of neighbors had rushed to his corner to see what the trouble in our neighborhood might be. They surrounded the reticent old man, attempting to comfort him, offering practical help. Would he come and stay with them for the night? Could they store any of his belongings? When the firefighters emerged from the basement to pronounce the trouble a broken steam pipe and not a fire, neighbors offered to help him clean up.

Finally reluctantly accepting the help of one of us more familiar to him to get settled for the night, he went back in. The firefighters took up their hoses and pulled away, and we all returned home.

Anthropologists say that throughout most of recorded time people have lived in clans and it was the clans, some say, that were the basic organism of society. People were created to function in small

groups, to come together to face troubles, to celebrate, to mourn. Although we modern people are supposed to be able to live independently, alone or in nuclear families, it is not actually possible to successfully live that way.

Neighborhoods are one vestige of the clan, a group in which one can find identity. Even if you live isolated on the margins of a neighborhood, it is your neighbors who show up both in times of tragedy and of joy.

Harrisburg is blessed by many things, but foremost among them is its many neighborhoods. Each tends to have its central meeting place — a café, a bar, a corner store, perhaps even the city's one remaining five-and-dime. Although neighborhoods may not seem active on the surface, all neighbors know where their neighborhood begins and ends. People generally do not walk their dogs beyond the boundaries of their own neighborhood. They get out of bed to investigate when fire trucks or ambulances stop in their own neighborhood. They talk about those neighbors who rarely — sometimes even never — appear in public. "It is when your neighbors are not gossiping about you that you have to worry," a psychiatrist once observed.

Neighborhoods are places where you walk. Downtown, people pass each other on the street on the way to work or to run errands, detouring around children on bicycles or playing ball in the street. In some neighborhoods, the street is lined with broad porches from which one can have conversations or merely nod to passers-by. Or the local style may involve knots of people hanging out on a street corner.

Neighborhoods can flourish, or they can die. Like most living things, they have their predators, chief among them automobiles and their associated public works. While a neighborhood might be able to absorb many small surface parking lots, perhaps softened by a few trees, one large out-of-scale parking garage may drown it. A hundred small businesses may make a city hum, but one shopping mall or self-contained office complex can leave a once-vibrant place a literal wasteland, despite the money it brings in.

Like other modern cities, Harrisburg is at a crossroads. Once economically devastated, its feeble pulse, restarted by a visionary and energetic mayor (fittingly once an emergency medical technician) has once again become strong. People are returning to the city streets at night, restaurants open, parks are replanted, a ball team plays under a summer sky.

If neighborhood block parties, cafes, bars, and even trouble-making activists flourish (Seattle gathered them into their own city department!),then Harrisburg can become a great city. Great enough not only to send fire trucks speeding to the rescue of one old man, but also to nurture the neighborhood fabric out of which neighborly concern and mutual help arise.
It is upon such occasions, in the middle of the night, that we can learn where we really live. *H*

LEFT PAGE: *Sweet Passions, now the Java House in the 1900 block of N. 3rd St., serves as a neighborhood meeting place.* ABOVE: *Flower boxes near Habitat for Humanity renovations on Zarker St. brighten the block.* BELOW: *Writer David Schwartz, his wife, Beth and son, join neighborhood member Tom Leonard at the North Street Cafe.*

BELOW: *Scott's Bar & Grill on Locust St. is a frequent rendevous location.* RIGHT: *Neighborhood organizations in Shipoke and other parts of the city keep their streets clean and crime free.* RIGHT PAGE TOP: *The 400 block of Walnut St. boutiques are very accessible to downtown residents as well as state capital employees.* RIGHT PAGE BOTTOM: *The Entrepreneur Group, formed to help neighborhood business-inclined youth, displays products at the African Family Festival.*

Harrisburg neighborhoods each show their own pride and characteristics. TOP LEFT TO BOTTOM: *1600 block of North St., Allison Hill; 1321 Green St., Midtown; 2810 block of N. 2nd St., Uptown; 1820 block of Regina St., Allison Hill.*

The City offers a wide variety of home environment options. **TOP TO BOTTOM LEFT:** *1900 block of Bellevue St., Allison Hill; Wilson Park; Front St., Shipoke*

Annually, the Historic Harrisburg Association sponsors a spring house and garden tour as well as a holiday house tour. Tours have included: FAR RIGHT: *the patio and swimming pool at the home of Karen and Jim Close at 3224 N. 3rd St.* BOTTOM: *the home at 2910 Parklane owned by Carol and Phil DiMartile.* BELOW: *the gardens and gazebo overlooking Italian Lake at Steven E. Dailey's home, 3021 Green St.* RIGHT: *Deborah Hughes' gardens on Herr St. in Midtown.*

RIGHT: *Former school teacher, James Cooper, performed much of the research and handiwork himself to restore the Uptown 6th St. firehouse to a favored restaurant, the Camp Curtin Barbecue Station.* BOTTOM RIGHT: *Many architecturally significant homes in Harrisburg await restoration.* BOTTOM LEFT: *Homeowners in many areas of Harrisburg maintain or restore their own homes.* LEFT: *In a program to upgrade schools and institute neighborhood K-8 classes, buildings including Shimmell School on S. 17th St. have been renovated.*

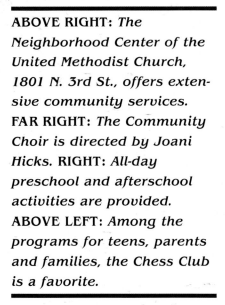

ABOVE RIGHT: *The Neighborhood Center of the United Methodist Church, 1801 N. 3rd St., offers extensive community services.* **FAR RIGHT:** *The Community Choir is directed by Joani Hicks.* **RIGHT:** *All-day preschool and afterschool activities are provided.* **ABOVE LEFT:** *Among the programs for teens, parents and families, the Chess Club is a favorite.*

ABOVE: *At the Mount Pleasant Hispanic American Center, 301 S. 13th St., Social Worker Jean Toro interviews Jenny Perez. The Center offers a wide range of counseling, medical and educational programs to the community.* RIGHT: *Angela M. Eline teaches children medical basics at the Center.*

BELOW: *In neighborhoods throughout Harrisburg, places of worship offer community services and religious instruction. The Beth El Temple is located in the Uptown at 2637 N. Front St. RIGHT: Former Beth El Rabbi Mark Greenspan and Cantor Paula A. Victor assist Ellen Greenberg as she holds the Torah at her Bat Mitzvah rehearsal.*

Chapter 6

In the Midst of Plenty

By John Hope

John Hope is a freelance writer and editor

Harrisburg, 1970. As I leave the South Bridge and start north on Second Street on my first house-hunting trip to the city, Harrisburg looks OK to me for two reasons: it has a job I want—working in the United Press International state capitol bureau as a reporter—and it's close to other places I like to go to: Philadelphia, where my family is; Pittsburgh, where we're moving from; Washington; New York City; the Jersey shore.

Harrisburg, 1999. As I leave the South Bridge and start north on Second Street toward our house, I'm reminded again how much I love this place I now call home and appreciate all that it has to offer.

Instead of moving to Washington with UPI as I had planned, I ended up staying here, working in a number of different jobs. My children grew up in the Harrisburg schools and have gone on to lives near and far. I served on the school board and have been active in religious and community organizations. Harrisburg is home.

Now, instead of looking to places hours away, I spend my time locally, finding new areas to explore, new wonders to appreciate.

When I worked for the Department of Environmental Resources in the 1970s, we opened a number of new state parks to help fulfill Secretary Maurice K. Goddard's dream of having one within 25 miles of every Pennsylvanian. I wrote the dedication speeches he gave and went to the ceremonies. As a result, I got to see Little Buffalo, Codorus, Locust Lake, and all the other parks in this area that bring us peace and recreation. We've camped at Pinchot and Caledonia, Cowan's Gap and Colonel Denning. And there still is nothing to compare with silently gliding in a canoe back into the channel off Pinchot lake or standing on the shore and fishing through yet another beautiful sunset.

When the kids were young, season passes to Hershey Park gave us a vacation at home. To me Hershey Park was a magical place at 10 p.m. as we rode the carousel for the last time, listening to its old-time band music, watching the drums play themselves. If we were lucky, there would be fireworks as we drove out of the park, once again full of good memories.

Trips to the Landis Valley Farm, Cornwall iron furnace, Strasburg railroad and other historical and cultural sites gave us a better understanding of the rich background the area has to offer.

Now that the kids are grown, I bike the rail trails at Stony Creek and York, and on Lancaster County's back roads, make regular trips to Gettysburg for the living history and Park Ranger programs, canoe and fish area streams and lakes, and in so many ways each year, appreciate where I live and what it gives me. And any time I need a lift, I go to Negley Park in Wormleysburg and look out over the beautiful skyline of Harrisburg, my home with so much to offer. *H*

FAR LEFT: *Harrisburg residents enjoy taking visitors to neighboring Lancaster's Amish country.* **ABOVE:** *Gettysburg National Military Park is about 30 miles south of Harrisburg just west of Route 15.* **LEFT:** *Fishermen try their luck on the South Branch of Codorus Creek, York Co.*

ABOVE: *Kayaks and canoes grace the Dauphin Narrows' rapids north of Harrisburg. The City has numerous recreational groups including canoe and bike clubs.* **TOP:** *A bicyclist enjoys his ride in Fishing Creek Valley.* **RIGHT:** *Skiing adventure is near Harrisburg at Ski Roundtop and other resorts.* **ABOVE RIGHT:** *A rock climber scales Pinnacle Rock at Pine Grove Furnace State Park.*

TOP: *The Penn National Race Course is just Northeast of Harrisburg.* ABOVE: *Historic Cornwall Furnace, administered by the state's Historical and Museum Commission, is nearby in Lebanon County.* ABOVE RIGHT: *the prestigious Dickinson College and Law School lies just to the southwest of Harrisburg in the town of Carlisle.* RIGHT: *The Wildcat rollercoaster is a recent addition to Hershey Park™.*

Chapter 7

The Government's Treasure Chest of Art
by Ruth Hoover Seitz

Ruth Hoover Seitz is a Harrisburg writer of books about Pennsylvania, including Pennsylvania's Capitol

In Harrisburg, state government matters. Every workday morning, approximately 20,000 employees converge on the city to serve the Commonwealth. They head to a number of state office buildings throughout the area to fill bureau and department slots. Some work in the Capitol itself, a "palace of art," as its architect, Joseph Huston, planned.

This treasure chest atop Capitol Hill is Harrisburg's link with classical Europe. St. Peter's Basilica in Rome inspired the overall design, which includes a dome similar to Michaelangelo's in the Vatican.

Other features of Pennsylvania's statehouse hark back to specific European venues. The design of the tile floor on the first floor is found in St. Mark's Cathedral in Venice. The ceilings in the legislative chambers resemble those of St. John Lateran in Rome, and the grand staircase looks like the marble one at the opera house in Paris. What was innovative during the Greek and Roman periods became a renaissance in 16th century Europe, and resurfaced as American beaux arts in the early 1900s.

Besides murals, medallions, and columns, the Capitol's decorative wall details—rosettes, urns, and other ornate motifs—are so prolific that a repeat visit is a must. Guided tours are offered seven days a week.

I return to the Capitol to experience its grandeur. What I enjoy most is the symbolic art—images and script—presented to tell Pennsylvania's history and to proclaim its ideals. The values of its founder, William Penn, and the development of the state stirred the commissioned artists—all Pennsylvanians—to create memorable paintings, stained glass, and sculpture. The art is a backdrop for a continually evolving workshop in government.

I feel a sense of awe whenever I enter the Capitol rotunda and lift my eyes to view sunlight and art mingling 272 feet up to the center of the dome. Edwin Austin Abbey, an internationally-respected imaginative Philadelphia artist, blended realism with symbolism. In four lunettes he depicted spirits guiding Pennsylvania's development. Angels in filmy robes contrast the gentle and feminine with vigorous physical exertion as they assist miners and steelworkers and oversee the ships of settlers and the flow of oil wells. In 1908, when these murals were installed, steel, oil, and coal were Pennsylvania's prime growth industries.

More of Abbey's work hangs in the chamber of the House of Representatives, whose elected members each represent approximately 59,000 citizens in 203 legislative districts. The oldest statewide organization, the House was founded shortly after Penn arrived in 1682. Penn put in place a representative body, "the people's choice," that would establish precedents for our nation. The House created the first Supreme Court, drafted the commonwealth's first Bill of Rights, and initiated the nation's first public school system. Founder Penn's sense of fairness resulted in his paying the first settlers for the land as documented in Abbey's mural "Penn's Treaty With the Indians." This realistic painting is paired with "Reading of the Declaration of Independence," another event of national significance.

Abbey's "The Apotheosis of Pennsylvania" dominates the view of the 203 representatives who sit in this chamber. Surrounded by gold leaf decorations over a deep blue wall and distinctive marble wainscoting, this mural features Genius of State, a female figure enthroned above 50 of the state's trailblazers in various fields. That all of the trailblazers honored are male is indicative of the 17th century's social order!

FAR LEFT: *Among its numerous projects, The Capitol Preservation Committee replaced the gold leaf and fully restored the Capitol dome and "Commonwealth", the female statue of mercy and justice by Roland Hinton Perry.* LEFT: *Complete restoration of the 1906 Capitol begun in 1982 included the cleaning of the Italian marble scupltures by George Grey Barnard at the West entrance.* ABOVE: *Inspired by Ghiberti's work in Florence, Italy, sculptor George Grey Barnard made the intricate designs for the bronze Capitol doors.*

In this chamber, as in that of the Senate, I like to observe the color details in the 24 stained glass windows, especially the shading of the folds of the clothing. Their artist, William B. Van Ingren, had studied under the great stained glass artists John LaFarge and Lewis C. Tiffany, who introduced him to opalescent glass.

One of the most prolific contributors to the Capitol's artwork was Violet Oakley, a dynamic artist with unshakable convictions. Among the stream of Capitol artisans, she was distinctive because she was a woman. Architect Huston hoped her commission would encourage other female artists.

Her artwork emerged from passionate ideals. Oakley deeply believed that William Penn's "Holy Experiment"—a government that gave religious freedom to all, that did not carry weapons, and that refused to fight—was a "17th century miracle" that could be duplicated. She put all her hope for the Commonwealth into a wide mural that spans the upper level of the Senate chamber. There, a lady in blue named "Utopia" washes away the evils of slavery and poverty in healing waters. Her strong physique is evident through her gossamer robes; she is as powerful as the love she symbolizes.

Oakley's other murals also depict history lessons that raise challenging ideals for government to follow. For example, in one Senate painting, "The Creation and Preservation of the Union," Abraham Lincoln sadly addresses the nation. Her artwork in the Governor's Reception Room portrays significant events in William Penn's life and the influences preceding it that led to his establishment of Pennsylvania. In the Supreme Court chamber, her "Book of Law" traces how international laws developed through civilization. The presentation includes graphics, text, and scenes, all marching around the wall like the pages of an illuminated manuscript.

In the Capitol, even the floor is art. I walk on Pennsylvania red clay fired into square tiles that make a pavement of earthy tones on the first floor. Among these floor tiles are hand-crafted mosaics of the state's inhabitants, including critters. They are the creation of Henry Chapman Mercer, an

FAR RIGHT: *One of the most impressive in the country, the Capitol's rotunda has recently been restored.* **ABOVE:** *Artist Violet Oakley's* Utopia *spans much of the upper front of the Senate Chamber.* **RIGHT:** *The House of Representatives Chamber is resplendent with chandeliers, gold leaf and artwork by Edwin Austin Abbey.*

133

archeologist–turned–ceramist who used his knowledge of the past to show how Pennsylvania was shaped by the work of thousands of hands. Some of the mosaics simply outline the rock carvings of Native Americans. Others show scenes of production—e.g., cooking apple butter or forging a chain—in complex designs with many pieces in the mosaic set together with cement bonds. The picture tiles tell the story of technology in chronological order, ending with the telephone and a 1908 Cadillac.

Outside, I like to pause at the entrance of the West Wing along Third Street and ponder the two gleaming white marble sculptures by George Grey Bernard. Universal in theme, the figures intertwine as do life's experiences—labor and rest, joy and sorrow. Among the friendly and forgiving figures of "Love and Labor" on the north side are a young man and woman stepping towards the future, chin up with optimism. Their hopeful stance uplifts me. No wonder Barnard's studio assistants called his statuary "the joys."

At the plaza in front of the award–winning East Wing along Commonwealth Avenue, I often stop my car and absorb the sound of the fountain water flowing into the pool. The computerized fountain's cycle creates a series of artful images of water against the classical lines of the Capitol.

No doubt the symbols and facts researched by the artists and integrated into their works are lost on many of the 80,000 people who tour the statehouse annually. Visitors are inspired by the overall impact of the 1906 building's magnificence. A guided tour and some time in the interactive Welcome Center enlarge their understanding of how state government works in this "palace of art." But the sense that they take with them is that they have had a brush with Renaissance Europe. The Capitol is the only place in Harrisburg that gives that sense. ℋ

BELOW: *An aerial view of the Capitol Complex places it in its setting – on a hill overlooking State St. and the Susquehanna River.* **RIGHT:** *The State Museum's Memorial Hall, the venue for many functions, holds an 18' statue of William Penn, a reproduction of the Penn Charter as well as the mural, The Vision of William Penn by Vincent Maragliotti.*

BOTTOM: *The State Museum of Pennsylvania's four floors of exhibit space include a Fine Arts Gallery, a 19th-century village, the Brockerhoff House, extensive industry/ technology, natural science/ecology and paleontology/geology exhibits. Bobcats in a Pennsylvania setting is one of the full-scale mammal dioramas.* BELOW: *The Native American Village stands next to the exhibits on archaeology and anthropology.*

BOTTOM: *Penn State Harrisburg serves the Harrisburg area at the Middletown campus. Both Temple University and Penn State also have downtown classrooms and Widener University's School of Law is located at 3800 Vartan Way.* BELOW: *The Dixon University Center, 2986 N. 2nd St., offers course work from many of the state universities.* RIGHT: *The Martin Luther King Government Center is conveniently located on Market Square.*

FAR RIGHT: *The Farm Show building's versatile arena is home to the professional soccer team, Harrisburg Heat, during the winter months.* BOTTOM: *Harrisburg's annual marathon begins on Commonwealth Avenue.* BELOW: *Fire trucks participated in the parade through Market Square to celebrate the 1998 Harrisburg Cougars state basketball championship.* RIGHT: *The annual Fire Apparatus Show and Muster is held along the Susquehanna River south of the Market St. Bridge.*

The Farm Show building is occupied year round with a vast variety of shows and exhibits including a circus, the PA Farm Show week events, boat, outdoor life, recreational vehicle, horse, and many other specialty exhibits. TOP: The annual Mennonite church sponsored Pennsylvania Quilt Auction at the Farm Show building raises money for disaster relief efforts around the world.
RIGHT: The Farm Show's outdoor auto market is a change to find a good auto buy.

BOTTOM: *Many performers and atten-ders at the wide variety of the Forum's concerts and programs remember the extraordinary 1800-seat auditorium by the elaborate portrayal of constellations on the 60' high ceiling.* LEFT: *Strawberry Square is a diverse mix of shops, spa-cious food court, restaurants, offices and atrium in a beautifully enclosed block of historic buildings. Climate con-trolled walkways connect the Square to the Hilton Hotel and the Whitaker Center.*

LEFT: *City Island, the home of the Harrisburg Senators, the Montreal Expos AA team, draws thousands on most summer weekends to its eating, marina and recreational facilities including Riverside Stadium. The Senators are six-time Eastern League champions ('87, '93, '96, '97, '98, '99)* BELOW: *Rascal, the Senators mascot, entertains the crowd at an evening game.*

JUN 2 7 2001

Celebrate Pennsylvania!

Featuring stunning color photos by Blair Seitz

www.celebratePA.com

PENNSYLVANIA'S CAPITOL takes you through this "Palace of Art" in Harrisburg. Enjoy the paintings, sculpture and stained glass. 8½" x 11" hc 80 photos $19.95

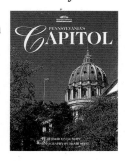

SUSQUEHANNA HEARTLAND shows you the reasons why the people of Harrisburg, York and Lancaster love living in the Susquehanna Valley. 8½" x 11" hc 180 photos $29.95

SAVE OUR LAND; SAVE OUR TOWNS lays out an easy-to-grasp blueprint for comunities to thrive while preserving the earth. 8½" x 11" p 150 photos $29.95

PHILADELPHIA AND ITS COUNTRYSIDE portrays historic and scenic attractions of Pennsylvania's Southeast. 8½" x 11" hc 180 photos $29.95

PITTSBURGH uncovers the distinctions of the Three Rivers City—its museums, its topography, its festivals. 8½" x 11" hc 125 photos $29.95

Insights Series
AMISH VALUES: WISDOM THAT WORKS describes how ten insights benefit these "plain people" and could enhance your life. 5½" x 8½" p color photos $9.95

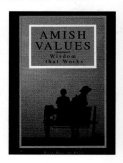

PENNSYLVANIA'S NATURAL BEAUTY invites you to the serene but wild beauty of Pennsylvania's state parks and forests—all four seasons. 8½" x 11" hc 120 photos $24.95

AMISH WAYS opens your window to Amish faith and culture through ordinary happenings. 8½"x 11" hc 150 photos $24.95

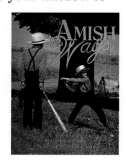

GETTYSBURG: CIVIL WAR MEMORIES takes you back to this battle as experienced by ten-year-old Charles McCurdy and other civilians. Photos of battle relics published for the first time. 5½" x 8½" p color photos $9.95

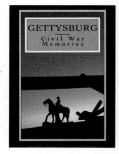

HANOVER PUBLIC LIBRARY HANOVER, PA.

PENNSYLVANIA'S TAPESTRY: SCENES FROM THE AIR will thrill you with aerial views of Pennsylvania's farms, forests, and waterways. 8½" x 11" hc 90 photos $24.95

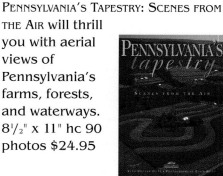

PENN STATE SPORTS STORIES AND MORE Master storyteller and former broadcaster Mickey Bergstein taps more than 50 years at Penn State to give a warm and touching insider's view of one of America's most notable universitites. Trade paperbacks: 300 pages; 20 B & W photos $19.95

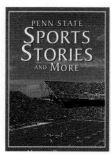

RB BOOKS™

"...richly beautiful"

available at your local bookstore or Call 1/800-497-1427 or from Harrisburg 232-7944
Call between 8:30 a.m. - 5:00 p.m. M-F or FAX: 717/238-3280 anytime